THE *Magna Book* OF

POT POURRI

AN IMAGINATIVE COLLECTION OF CREATIVE IDEAS TO MAKE AND DISPLAY POT POURRI

Disclaimer
Care should be taken when preparing pot pourri.
Some ingredients might cause an allergic reaction.
Neither the author nor the publisher can be
held responsible for any adverse reactions to the
pot pourri ingredients discussed within.

Editor: Fleur Robertson
Editorial Assistance: Kirsty Wheeler
Original Design Concept: Peter Bridgewater
Design: Stonecastle Graphics Ltd
Photography: Richard Paines
Additional photography: Linda Burgess and Stonecastle Graphics Ltd
Production Director: Gerald Hughes
Production: Ruth Arthur, Sally Connolly, Neil Randles
Typesetting: Julie Smith

Jacket photograph: Richard Paines

CLB 3132
This 1994 edition published by Magna Books,
Magna Road, Wigston, Leicester LE18 4ZH
© 1993 CLB Publishing Ltd
Godalming, Surrey, England.
Printed and bound in Singapore.
All rights reserved.
ISBN 1 85422 549 9

THE *Magna Book* OF
POT
POURRI

MARY LAWRENCE

MAGNA
BOOKS

History

The ancient Egyptians relied heavily on the wonderful properties of perfume. Flowers and fragrances influenced their leisure, medicine, religion and even their architecture – indeed, they were the most extravagant users of scented materials in the ancient world. It is said that Cleopatra covered the floors of her apartments with a deep layer of rose petals and had pillows stuffed with them to entice Mark Antony. Egyptian palaces and great houses were adorned with scented flowers and large containers of pot pourri, while the latter were also buried with the dead.

On the other side of the Mediterranean, the Greeks also used flowers and herbs in religious and civil ceremonies and their houses were built to look out onto gardens of flowers and fragrant herbs. Small bags of pot pourri would be thoughtfully placed behind individual guests at banquets to welcome them.

By 1 BC, flowers had become a part of Roman life. They were used to adorn homes, temples, and civic buildings, and even the streets for triumphal processions. Romans wore flowers in their hair, strewed floors with herbs, valued roses highly and even decorated their food with them. Sweet-smelling flowers were burnt as offerings to the gods, from which we have the word 'perfume', the Latin for 'through smoke'.

History

By the twelfth century, western travellers had reached the Far East and brought back a huge fund of information on new plants and spices. They also knew of the art of distillation and the isolation of essential oils developed in Arabia.

During the Middle Ages the foundations of the current use of flowers, spices and oils were laid and by the 1500s the perfume industry had begun. Queen Elizabeth had gardens of scented plants created for her pleasure, and ladies at the English court started to make perfumed toiletries. The fashion for fragrant pot pourri grew. Soon all large houses had gardens with areas set aside to grow flavouring herbs, medicinal plants and others for use in toilet preparations. In these

10

houses there would be a still room, housing one or more small units for distillation. It was a warm room where herbs and flowers were hung to dry, and seeds, spices, roots, fixatives and oils were kept. Pot pourris, 'sweet bags' and lotions were prepared there.

In Victorian times pot pourri was still popular, though often bought ready mixed. Beautiful porcelain or pottery pot pourri bowls, open and perforated, were made in the eighteenth and nineteenth centuries. But the pastime was still a pleasure reserved for the leisured: it would be another century before the average person would have the time to rediscover the joys of flower perfumes and the delights of making pot pourri.

The Magic of Scent

Smell is one of the most important of our senses. Primitive man's was very highly developed, and was essential to his survival. Our sense of smell is several hundred times greater than our sense of taste, but modern times have lead to a decline in our use of this ability: for instance, we now rely more on our eyes to detect the freshness of food than on our more trustworthy noses.

Smell is very individual, and no two people agree about a scent, but often an aroma will conjure memories of past occasions. Scent is often compared with musical terms and thought as notes in a scale – the 'high notes' will be the sharp smells like citrus, the middle levels the sweeter tones of roses and the lower ones the warm and musky tones of spices.

When preparing blends of pot pourri, the sharp smell in the peel of lemons, oranges and limes can be retained by rolling them in orris root powder and drying slowly in a very low oven. Stored in an airtight container, they can be used whole or ground down, depending on the recipe. The great variety in the middle tones comes from highly scented flowers like carnations, honeysuckle, jasmine, lavender, lilies, mock orange and that most fragrant of flowers, the rose, prized since antiquity for this virtue. The lower notes of spices and woods are best found in cinnamon sticks, ginger root, cedar chips, cloves, sandalwood, nutmeg pieces and allspice.

Ingredients

Plant Materials

When making pot pourri, a wide variety in the texture and colour of the flowers, leaves and additives is of great importance. Preserve a good selection of flowers and leaves by picking them at their best and laying them out on newspaper in a dry, sheltered place, or tying them in bunches and hanging them upside down in a warm, dark, airy room. Dry to a papery feel. When dry, discard the stems and any damaged material and store them in airtight containers until they are required. For pot pourri, it is best to pick herbs in their flowering season. Rosemary, thyme, lavender, nepeta and bay have a traditional, as well as practical, use in a blend.

Essential Oils

Because so many of our modern varieties of flowers have been bred for looks rather than perfume, most modern pot pourri recipes require the additional use of plant essential oils. These

14

are extracted or distilled: it requires enormous quantities of flowers to produce a small phial of perfume oil. Essential oils are extremely powerful and volatile and so must be used with great care when blending. They should be added one drop at a time to the correct amount, or the delicate balance sought will be lost. Always buy very good quality essential oils and store them in dark bottles with tight-fitting caps. Wear rubber gloves when handling them to avoid contamination.

Fixatives

To retain the scent within a pot pourri a fixative must be added. Orris root powder is used most often and can be obtained from chemists or specialist shops. It can be made from the older fleshy roots of *Iris florentina* peeled, chopped, dried and then ground with a pestle and mortar. Other fixatives, some of which are scented, include myrrh, sandalwood, tonka bean, frankincense, oakmoss and gum benzoin.

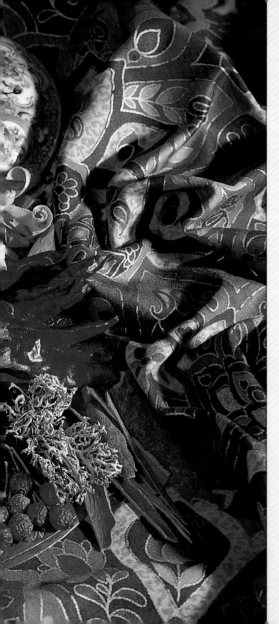

S*pices*

Spices add warmth and relish to a pot pourri, and also act as a fixative. They bring gusto to a gentleman's mixture, and a seasonal touch to a Christmas blend. Spices are bought whole and freshly crushed or ground for a particular blend. Whole spices like vanilla pods, tiny chillies, nutmeg, juniper berries, red and green peppercorns, cardamom seeds, rose-hips and oakmoss will all add seductive texture to a mix.

A Spicy Blend
1 cup verbena leaves
1 cup bay leaves
1 cup small chillies
8 whole nutmegs
1 cup sandalwood shavings
4 tbsp allspice
4 tbsp crushed cinnamon bark
1 cup beech nut husks
2 tbsp orris root powder
4 drops sandalwood essential oil

17

Essential Oils

Oil	Scent
Bay	*spicy*
Bergamot	*orange*
Cajuput	*camphorous*
Chamomile	*apple*
Clary sage	*musky*
Geranium	*light musk*
Lavender	*fresh, sharp*
Melissa	*lemony*
Neroli	*sweet*
Patchouli	*strong camphorous*
Rose	*sweet, strong*
Otto of roses	*heavy, sweet*
Rosemary	*refreshing*
Sandalwood	*sweet, woody*
Verbena	*lemony*
Vetiver	*sweet*
Ylang-ylang	*heavy, flowery*

The Oil Burner

By heating essential oils their capricious fragrance will be released to sweeten the air. This practice dates back to ancient Greek times and has been used through out the centuries to fumigate homes and protect against disease. In recent years little ceramic oil burners (really a misnomer, as the oil is heated and not usually allowed to burn) have become very popular for use in the home. A small amount of water is placed in the top depression and a few drops of favourite oil added. The oil, heated by a night-light candle, evaporates, gently scenting the air.

Making Pot Pourri

There are two methods of making pot pourri: the moist and the dry. The moist method uses damask rose petals for a long-lasting, sweetly scented mix, but the easier method for a prettier mix is the dry. Note: do not use wooden utensils as these absorb oils.

The Dry Method Measure the materials into a bowl and stir gently. Transfer to a tight-lidded container and seal. Leave for 3 to 4 weeks to mature, shaking occasionally. Use as desired.

'New Rose' Blend
4 cups dried rose petals
2 cups miniature rose buds
2 cups dried lavender flowers
1 cup lemon verbena leaves
1 chopped vanilla pod (bean)
1 tsp ground cinnamon
4 tbsp orris root powder
2 drops rose essential oil
roses and astrantia for decoration

20

The Moist Method Dry scented cabbage and damask rose heads until they are leathery in texture. Pack 3 cups of their petals into a straight-sided crock and cover with a cup of non-ionised salt. Layer rose petals and salt until the crock is half full. Cover with a weight on a saucer. Stir the mix each day for 10 days, pouring off excess liquid. Store for a month. Break up the caked mixture and display in a container with a perforated lid or use it for the following mix.

'Old Rose' Blend

9 cups dried caked mixture
2 chopped vanilla pods
½ tbsp ground cinnamon
½ tbsp crushed cloves
4 tbsp orris root powder
2 drops rose essential oil (optional)

Stir and seal in an airtight container. Store for 4 weeks, shaking occasionally, and then use.

A Sundae Glass

Extra fun in making pot pourri is had in searching out attractive display containers which will compliment the mixture. This elegant sundae glass, for example, makes a perfect, if unusual, display for a summer buffet table.

The dried flowers of white statice, blue larkspur, pink larkspur and pink globe amaranth together with a chopped vanilla pod are layered in the glass, colour by colour, to resemble ice cream. The final layers are firmed down using the base of a tumbler. Finish this summery design with a frothy looking pale pink dried peony for a delicate and 'delicious' final touch.

A Decorated Basket

One of the finest ways to display pot pourri is in a basket that has been decorated with dried flowers. Line a basket with plastic and using a glue gun, position the dried flowers around the edge. Fill the completed basket with pot pourri.

A Winter Blend

1 cup lemon verbena

1 cup rosemary

½ cup cedar wood chippings

1 oz oak moss

1 cup rosehips

1 cup mixed orange and lemon peel

1 cup assorted small cones

½ cup small red chillies

½ cup lichen

10 whole and 10 crushed juniper berries

2 tbsp cloves

2 tbsp ground allspice

2 drops each of pine, clove and lemon oil

¼ cup orris root powder

Flower Frieze

This fragrant pressed flower collage is an eye-catching way to perfume a room. A piece of thick blue cardboard is overlaid with a sheet of textured paper to give a 'high summer' background and the pressed flowers arranged on it as an abundant garden border. The flowers and foliage are fixed with a little latex adhesive on their undersides. Use tweezers to position and create the design.

Make up a sachet by placing 2 tablespoons of Summer Dawn Blend (see p 50) in the centre of a square of muslin, add 2 drops of essential oil to strengthen the perfume and tie the sachet. Place it in a box with the flower frieze, seal and leave for 4 weeks to perfume the collage. If the frieze is framed, tape the sachet to the back and add to it a few drops of the relevant essential oil.

Drawer Fresheners

Make a bag to scent a linen closet by gathering some pot pourri in a lace-edged handkerchief and tying it with a bow. Alternatively sew and fill closely woven material shapes as shown here for drawer fresheners, sticks and sachets.

A Blend for Pouches and Shapes
1 cup rose petals
1 cup lemon balm leaves and flowers
½ cup rosemary leaves
2 tbsp powdered lemon peel
1 tsp ground cumin
2 tsp orris root powder
5 drops rose essential oil

28

A 'Masculine' Mix for Stick Drawer Fresheners
½ cup curry plant leaves
½ cup lemon verbena leaves
½ cup bay leaves
2 tsp ground cumin
2 tsp oris root powder
3 drops bay essential oil

A Blend for Anti-Moth Bags
1 cup tansy leaves
1 cup wormwood leaves
1 cup lavender
½ cup rosemary leaves
2 tsp orris root powder

Victorian Brooch Cushion

Victorian ladies displayed their brooches on pads, and it was fashionable to make cushions filled with pot pourri for this so the perfume was released each time a pin was fixed or withdrawn. This cushion of velvet and old lace was lined with wadding to give a firm shape before being filled with a fine-ground, strongly fragranced pot pourri.

A 'Nostalgic' Pot Pourri
1 cup lavender
1 cup rosemary
½ cup scented pelargonium leaves
½ cup mint
½ cup marjoram
oris powder
2 tsp ground cloves
2 drops lavender essential oil
1 drop rosemary essential oil

Mix everything in a container with a tight lid and mature for 2 weeks before using as the filling.

30

Gentleman's Relish

2 tsp cumin seeds

2 tbsp mixed peppercorns

3 tbsp cloves

2 tbsp japonica

1 tbsp cardamom

4 tbsp small red chillies

2 cups marigold petals

1 cup marrow seeds

1 tbsp star anise

1 inch length ginger root

4 cinnamon sticks

1 tbsp mixed lemon and orange peel

a few dried apple slices and small cones

This spicy pot pourri will add a cultivated aroma to a man's room. Place the first five ingredients in a bowl and mix. Remove 2 tablespoons and grind with a pestle and mortar. Return this to the bowl and mix in the other ingredients. Store sealed for 4 weeks. Display in a wooden box and use the apple slices and cones to decorate.

Therapeutic Cushions

Pot pourri mixtures can be blended to include plants with therapeutic properties — most effective if added to pillows or cushions. Since Roman times the soporific effect of dried hop flowers has lead to their being stuffed into pillows, where their gentle aroma has helped the insomniac to a restful night's sleep. The best way to use these mixes is to grind them into a coarse powder and sew them into a muslin sachet which can then be placed inside the cushion case or pillow.

A Blend to Refresh and Ease Anxiety
1 cup scented geranium leaves
2 cups lavender flowers
2 cups ground grapefruit peel
2 tsp orris root powder
2 drops bergamot essential oil

A Blend to Benefit Breathing*
1 cup eucalyptus leaves
1 cup peppermint leaves
½ cup rosemary leaves
½ cup scented geranium leaves
1 cup chopped basil
2 tsp orris root powder
3 drops eucalyptus essential oil

A Blend to Clear a Headache
½ cup peppermint leaves
2 cups lavender flowers
2 cups chamomile flowers
2 tsp orris root powder
1 drop lavender essential oil
2 drops peppermint essential oil

*In the photograph, this blend is in a flower
shape fixed to the cushion with velcro so that
it can be moved as desired.

Highland Pomander

The original French 'pomme d'ambre' was a lump of ambergris roughly the size of a crab apple. In the Middle Ages these were placed in carved ivory or silver cases and hung from the belt or the neck to protect the wearer from infection. A citrus pomander was favoured by Cardinal Wolsey who always hung one round his neck when visiting the sick. Here, the stimulating smell of the cloves and the orange is matched by the striking tartan ribbon hanging.

Small orange, lemon or lime

cloves

masking tape

tartan ribbon

cocktail stick

1 tsp each of ground cumin, nutmeg, ginger and orris root powder

Use the tape to divide the fruit into quarters and mark the position of the ribbon. Prick all over the remaining part of the fruit with a cocktail stick or thin knitting needle – this will make it easier to press in the cloves.

Using a thimble, press the stalk end of the cloves into each quarter of the fruit until it is loosely studded: the fruit will shrink a little as it dries and the cloves will meet up. Make up the mix of ground spices and orris root powder and pour it into a strong bag. Roll the clove-studded fruit around in the bag to cover it with the powder mixture. Set aside for several weeks to dry, occasionally shaking it gently. When the fruit is hard, brush off the surplus powder. Fold and tie lengths of ribbon to fit the pomander. Make a hanging loop and glue it to the top with a bow. Feather a length of ribbon into a tassel and glue it to the pomander base for a final flourish.

Hearts and Roses

small heart-shaped cake baking tin
florist's dry foam
glue or pins, needle and white cotton
1-inch-wide broderie anglais ribbon 4 times
longer than the circumference of the tin
2 handfuls of miniature rosebud pot pourri
rose essential oil

A pretty pomander can be made using rosebuds
with dried flower foam in the shape of a heart.

Shape the foam to fit the tin and trim flush.
Take half of the ribbon and gather the inside
edges to make a frill around the outside of the tin.
Secure with pins. Make a second frill and secure
it an inch inside the first. Starting at the outside
edge, push rosebuds into the foam following the
heart shape until it is filled solid with rosebuds.
Glue in rosebuds between the frills to form an
outer heart. Now add to the fragrance with a few
drops of rose essential oil just on the centre buds.

Lavender Garland

wire wreath frame
large quantity of long-stalked lavender
thin vine branches
elastic bands, string and glue gun
dried flowers and ribbon to decorate

Pick fresh lavender with long stems. Remove the flowers to dry for other pot pourri use. Divide the stems into bunches, securing top and bottom with elastic bands. Start by tying the first bunch head to an inside edge of the frame, twist the bunch diagonally across the top and under the base and fix temporarily with string. Fix the second bunch beside the first with the glue gun. Twist this bunch around the frame following the line of the first bunch for an even 'rope' effect until the wreath is finished. Secure the back using the glue gun. Finish binding with vine branches and decorate with flowers and ribbon. This long-lasting wreath can be refreshed by squeezing it to release the lavender oil retained in the stems.

Scented Notepaper

The scented notepaper here may seem an extravagant collection of stationery, but it has been made economically with the help of pot pourri and a few pressed flowers.

Choose handmade or artist paper with a pleasing texture. Decide on the size of the paper or card required and divide up the large sheets by folding a line at the desired position to divide the sheet, open it up again and lay a steel rule along the fold line and carefully tear against it, giving the appearance of a 'deckle' edge. Arrange the pressed flowers with a touch of latex adhesive and protect them by covering with special protective film or melted wax.

To perfume the plain and decorated paper, place it in a box with a tight-fitting lid containing a sachet of ground *'New Rose' Blend* pot pourri (see p20) which must be strengthened with 2 drops of rose essential oil. Leave this for 4 to 6 weeks for the paper to take up the perfume.

Pot Pourri Baths

For a relaxing, skin-softening bath, add to it a pot pourri sachet containing equal parts of the following: organic oatmeal, wheat bran and dried whole milk powder. To each 2 cups of this add ¼ cup each of chopped and dried lavender and rosemary. Mix all the ingredients in a bowl and use 2 tablespoons of the mixture for each sachet. Sew a long ribbon to each sachet so they can be hung from the running taps if desired.

'Start of the Day' Footbath

If the prospect of a long day on your feet seems daunting, soak them for 10 to 15 minutes in this therapeutic bath and the revitalising elements will quickly refresh and energise the whole body. The recipe is very easy.

570ml/1 pint cider vinegar
570ml/1 pint mineral water
4 tbsp baby shampoo
20 drops lavender essential oil
20 drops lemongrass essential oil
3 drops food colouring (optional)

Pour the cider, water, oils and food colouring into a bottle and shake vigorously for a minute. Add the baby shampoo and store in a refrigerator. To use, shake and add half a cup to a hot footbath.

A Pot Pourri of Sea Shells

Having spent many weeks removing the moisture from the flowers and leaves of a pot pourri mixture it would be a great mistake to display it in a steamy bathroom where it would re-absorb moisture and risk mould attack. Solve this problem by perfuming sea shells. Their distinctive appearance will enhance a bathroom shelf while giving off a sharp and refreshing aroma.

Desert Island Blend
a selection of sea shells
1 sheet of blotting paper
bay, melissa, sandalwood and
cypress essential oils

Scrub the shells and soak them overnight in a weak solution of household bleach. Then rinse them in fresh water until the bleach smell has gone. Leave them to dry in an airing cupboard for 3 days. On the blotting paper, place 10 drops of bay and 5 each of the other essential oils. Place the paper in a tight-lidded plastic container to make an infusion box. Leave the shells in this for 3 weeks, after which they are ready to display. To renew their perfume, return them to the box.

A Pot Pourri of Cones

Blended with spices and oils, pine cones give a seasonal aroma to a room, especially when thrown on an open fire to release a burst of fragrance.

Pine Forest Blend
a mixed selection of cones
2 tbsp cloves
1 tbsp ground cumin
1 tbsp sliced stem ginger
6 drops clove essential oil
6 drops sandalwood essential oil
1 tbsp orris root powder

Clean and dry the cones and place in a small bin liner. Mix the other ingredients, add them to the bag and seal. Set aside for 6 weeks, shaking the contents occasionally. Then remove the cones, shake them, and arrange them on a pretty display dish, adding a bunch of cinnamon sticks and a bow for decoration. Add more cones to the bag to supply the display with ready replacements.

Seasonal Blends

Pressed forget-me-nots and tiny heartsease violas will add much visual character to this recipe, with its sweet, fresh smell of early summer.

The combination of scents used in this blend will cheer any winter day with the smells of a summer evening walk through a freshly mown hayfield.

Summer Dawn Blend

3 cups pink larkspur flowers

3 cups blue delphinium flowers

2 cups clover heads

2 cups clove carnation petals

2 cups lemon verbena leaves

2 cups strawberry leaves

2 tbsp ground lemon peel

1 cup orris root powder

10 drops neroli essential oil

10 drops geranium essential oil

Thanksgiving Blend

2 cups chamomile flowers and leaves

2 cups melilot flowers and leaves

3 cups marigold petals

2 cups lemon verbena leaves

1 cup golden potentilla flowers

½ cup orris root powder

5 drops each of chamomile, clary sage, sandalwood essential oils

a handful of oakmoss and cones to decorate

Pot Pourri Flowers

Plants to grow in the flower garden for drying to
build up a store of pot pourri basic materials.

Scent	Colour	Texture
Clove carnation	Astrantia	Amaranth
Daphne	Buttercup	Clover flowers
Damask rose	Cornflower	Bells of Ireland
Dianthus	Delphinium	Elderflower
Freesia	Forget-me-not	Hops
Honeysuckle	Helichrysum	Hydrangea
Hops	Larkspur	Lady's mantle
Jonquil	Marigold	Nigella seedheads
Lilac	Montbretia	Peony
Lily of the valley	Nigella	Pearl everlasting
Marigold	Pansy	Poppy seedheads
Mock orange	Sun spurge	Potentilla
Pelargonium	Viola	Rose hip
Violet	Yarrow	Zinnia

Pot Pourri Herbs

All these herbs can be used to good effect in pot pourri mixtures, being as important to many blends as flowers. Indeed, the flowers of some herbs rival in beauty those in the flower border.

Angelica – leaves and roots
Basil – leaves
Bay – leaves
Bergamot – leaves and red flowers
Borage – blue flowers
Dill – yellow flowers
Chamomile – leaves and yellow-centred flowers
Coriander – seeds
Fennel – yellow flowers
Feverfew – small yellow-and-white flowers,

Hyssop – leaves and purple or pink flowers
Lavender – purple or mauve flowers
Lemon balm – leaves
Lemon verbena – leaves
Nepeta – leaves
Meadowsweet – leaves and creamy flowers
Myrtle – leaves and yellow flowers
Peppermint – leaves
Rosemary – leaves
Santolina – leaves and yellow flowers
Soapwort – small pink flowers
Sweet marjoram – leaves
Tansy – leaves and flowers
Thyme – leaves and flowers
Woodruff – leaves

55

Special Properties

When growing or blending plants or their fruit for use in pot pourri, it is as well to understand some of their useful and healing properties. Be aware that the juices and essential oils of these plants can enter the body by inhalation and by skin contact – for example, the scent of a crushed clove of garlic rubbed on the sole of the foot is very soon detected on the breath!

CHAMOMILE As it is a natural tranquilliser, make tisanes in the evening from dried chamomile flowers to ensure a good night's sleep, and use them in a bedroom pot pourri. Bath bags of chamomile will calm nerves and soothe bath-shy children. It can also be used to treat skin problems.

LAVENDER Lavender has always been associated with toiletries. Oil of lavender was carried by the Roman legions to heal sore feet, bruises, burns and war wounds. It is a natural antiseptic, promoting healing and minimising scarring.

EUCALYPTUS A pot pourri with a strong base of eucalyptus leaves is a must when the household is attacked by chest colds. Used as an inhalant, the essential oil will assist all bronchial problems. It also finds favour as an insect repellent.

GERANIUM PELARGONIUM CAPITATUM This is the most common variety of the scented geranium family. The crushed leaves release a wonderful spicy lemon scent. Crushed dried leaves make a fine addition to a bath bag pot pourri mixture: the fresh leaves used in this way leave the skin radiant. The essential oil, when much diluted with almond oil, heals chilblains.

THYME This herb has an enduring perfume in its dried form, though needs to be crushed occasionally to release its scent. Up to and during the 1914-18 war, a preparation of it was used widely as an antiseptic for soldiers' wounds: it has a very soothing effect and promotes recovery.

ROSEMARY A handful boiled in a pint of water, cooled and strained, is one of the best hair conditioners. Fresh leaves made into a bath bag creates a most stimulating bath to start the day, while the essential oil is good for muscular pains.

PEPPERMINT This herb brings a lovely crisp and minty touch to pot pourris. Crushed, the dried leaves make a tisane to aid digestion. Peppermint also aids circulation, is an antiseptic and repels many insects, such as aphids.

Flower Language

In the eighteenth century, while in Turkey, Lady Wortley Montague collated a list of the symbolic meanings of flowers, which were part of local tradition. Once published in England, the idea spread, and posies that were, in effect, messages became the rage. Here are the meanings attached to some of the flowers we use in pot pourri.

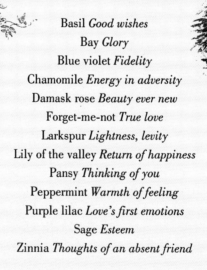

Basil *Good wishes*
Bay *Glory*
Blue violet *Fidelity*
Chamomile *Energy in adversity*
Damask rose *Beauty ever new*
Forget-me-not *True love*
Larkspur *Lightness, levity*
Lily of the valley *Return of happiness*
Pansy *Thinking of you*
Peppermint *Warmth of feeling*
Purple lilac *Love's first emotions*
Sage *Esteem*
Zinnia *Thoughts of an absent friend*

Acknowledgements

The publishers would like to thank the following for permission to reproduce:

Bridgeman Art Library, London, with acknowledgements to the Archaelogical Museum, Naples, for 1st-century wall painting of a maiden gathering flowers, p. 9.

Fine Art Photographic Library, London, for *A Symphony in Pink*/Ricci, p. 10; *Pot Pourri*/Johnson, p. 11; *In a Cottage Garden*/Strachen, p. 53; *A Posy of Pretty Flowers*/Bauerle, p. 54; *Poppy Girl*/Kendrick, p. 59.

The Garden Picture Library, London, for title page/ facing page (Linda Burgess).

The Iris Hardwick Library of Photographs, Sherborne, for pp. 54-55 (background) and p. 55 (oval inset).

Suppliers
Mary Lawrence, Swan Craft Gallery
Ashfield-cum-Thorpe, Stowmarket
Suffolk, England IP14 6LU
The gallery runs a mail order service for items
for pressed flower and pot pourri work.